YOU ARE GOD'S MASTERPIECE

A journal to draw you nearer to God

DEDICATION

To Annabeth and Millie
May you always know how loved you are.

CONTENTS

1 YOU ARE A NEW CREATION   Pg 7

2 YOU ARE FORGIVEN   Pg 11

3 YOU ARE COMPLETE   Pg 15

4 YOU ARE SECURE   Pg 19

5 YOU ARE FREE   Pg 23

6 YOU ARE CAPABLE   Pg 27

7 YOU ARE WONDERFULLY MADE   Pg 31

8 YOU ARE GOD'S WORKMANSHIP   Pg 35

9 YOU ARE WELCOME IN GOD'S PRESENCE   Pg 39

10 YOU ARE HIDDEN IN CHRIST   Pg 43

11 YOU ARE CHRIST'S FRIEND   Pg 47

12 YOU ARE GOD'S HEIR   Pg 51

13 YOU ARE AN OVERCOMER   Pg 55

14 YOU ARE CHOSEN   Pg 59

15 YOU ARE GOD'S CHILD   Pg 63

16 YOU ARE NOT ALONE   Pg 67

17 YOU ARE FRUITFUL   Pg 71

18 YOU HAVE AN ETERNAL HOME   Pg 75

   ABOUT THE AUTHOR   Pg 79

YOU ARE A NEW CREATION

I AM A NEW CREATION

The bible says:

"Therefore, if anyone is in Christ, he is a new creation. The old has passed away; behold, the new has come."

2 Corinthians 5:17 (ESV)

Sometimes I believe…

But this verse teaches me…

Prayer Points

God, thank you that…

God, please help me…

Doodle space

If you drew your thoughts, what would they look like?

YOU ARE
FORGIVEN

I AM FORGIVEN

The bible says:

"For by the blood of Christ we are set free, that is, our sins are forgiven. How great is the grace of God."

Ephesians 1:7 (GNT)

Sometimes I believe…

But this verse teaches me…

Prayer Points

God, thank you that…

God, please help me…

Doodle space

If you drew your thoughts, what would they look like?

YOU ARE COMPLETE

I AM COMPLETE

The bible says:

"For in Christ lives all the fullness of God in a human body. So you also are complete through your union with Christ, who is the head over every ruler and authority."

Colossians 2:9-10 (NLT)

Sometimes I believe…

But this verse teaches me…

Prayer Points

God, thank you that…

God, please help me…

Doodle space

If you drew your thoughts, what would they look like?

YOU ARE SECURE

I AM SECURE

The bible says:

"For I am convinced that neither death nor life, neither angels nor demons, neither the present nor the future, nor any powers, neither height nor depth, nor anything else in all creation, will be able to separate us from the love of God that is in Christ Jesus our Lord."

Romans 8:38-39 (NIV)

Sometimes I believe…

But this verse teaches me…

Prayer Points

God, thank you that…

God, please help me…

Doodle space

If you drew your thoughts, what would they look like?

YOU ARE FREE

I AM FREE

The bible says:

"You have been set free from sin and have become slaves to righteousness."

Romans 6:18 (NIV)

Sometimes I believe…

But this verse teaches me…

Prayer Points

God, thank you that…

God, please help me…

Doodle space

If you drew your thoughts, what would they look like?

YOU ARE CAPABLE

I AM CAPABLE

The bible says:

"I can do all this through him who gives me strength."

Philippians 4:13 (NIV)

Sometimes I believe…

But this verse teaches me…

Prayer Points

God, thank you that…

God, please help me…

Doodle space

If you drew your thoughts, what would they look like?

YOU ARE WONDERFULLY MADE

I AM WONDERFULLY MADE

The bible says:

"For you created my inmost being; you knit me together in my mother's womb. I praise you because I am fearfully and wonderfully made; your works are wonderful; I know that full well."

Psalm 139:13-14 (NIV)

Sometimes I believe…

But this verse teaches me…

Prayer Points

God, thank you that…

God, please help me…

Doodle space

If you drew your thoughts, what would they look like?

YOU ARE GOD'S WORKMANSHIP

I AM GOD'S WORKMANSHIP

The bible says:

"For we are his workmanship, created in Christ Jesus for good works, which God prepared beforehand, that we should walk in them.

Ephesians 2:10 (ESV)

Sometimes I believe…

But this verse teaches me…

Prayer Points

God, thank you that…

God, please help me…

Doodle space

If you drew your thoughts, what would they look like?

YOU ARE WELCOME IN GOD'S PRESENCE

I AM WELCOME IN GOD'S PRESENCE

The bible says:

"So let us come boldly to the throne of our gracious God. There we will receive his mercy, and we will find grace to help us when we need it most."

Hebrews 4:16 (NLT)

Sometimes I believe…

But this verse teaches me…

Prayer Points

God, thank you that…

God, please help me…

Doodle space

If you drew your thoughts, what would they look like?

YOU ARE HIDDEN IN CHRIST

I AM HIDDEN IN CHRIST

The bible says:

"Think about the things of heaven, not the things of earth. For you died to this life, and your real life is hidden with Christ in God. And when Christ, who is your life, is revealed to the whole world, you will share in all his glory."

Colossians 3:3 (NLT)

Sometimes I believe…

But this verse teaches me…

Prayer Points

God, thank you that…

God, please help me…

Doodle space

If you drew your thoughts, what would they look like?

YOU ARE CHRIST'S FRIEND

I AM CHRIST'S FRIEND

The bible says:

" I no longer call you servants because a servant does not know his master's business. Instead, I have called you friends, for all that I have heard from my Father I have made known to you,"

John 15:15 (NIV)

Sometimes I believe…

But this verse teaches me…

Prayer Points

God, thank you that…

God, please help me…

Doodle space

If you drew your thoughts, what would they look like?

YOU ARE
GOD'S HEIR

I AM GOD'S HEIR

The bible says:

"Now if we are children, then we are heirs – heirs of God and co-heirs with Christ"

Romans 8:17 (NIV)

Sometimes I believe…

But this verse teaches me…

Prayer Points

God, thank you that…

God, please help me…

Doodle space

If you drew your thoughts, what would they look like?

YOU ARE
AN
OVERCOMER

I AM AN OVERCOMER

The bible says:

"In all these things we have complete victory through him who loved us!"

Romans 8:37 (GNT)

Sometimes I believe…

But this verse teaches me…

Prayer Points

God, thank you that…

God, please help me…

Doodle space

If you drew your thoughts, what would they look like?

YOU ARE CHOSEN

I AM CHOSEN

The bible says:

"For we know, brothers and sisters, loved by God, that he has chosen you."

1 Thessalonians 1:4 (NIV)

Sometimes I believe…

But this verse teaches me…

Prayer Points

God, thank you that…

God, please help me…

Doodle space

If you drew your thoughts, what would they look like?

YOU ARE
GOD'S CHILD

I AM GOD'S CHILD

The bible says:

"Yet to all who did receive him, to those who believed in his name, he gave the right to become children of God."

John 1:12 (NIV)

Sometimes I believe…

But this verse teaches me…

Prayer Points

God, thank you that…

God, please help me…

Doodle space

If you drew your thoughts, what would they look like?

YOU ARE
NOT ALONE

I AM NOT ALONE

The bible says:

"God has said, "Never will I leave you; never will I forsake you."
Hebrews 13:5 (NIV)

Sometimes I believe…

But this verse teaches me…

Prayer Points

God, thank you that…

God, please help me…

Doodle space

If you drew your thoughts, what would they look like?

YOU ARE
FRUITFUL

I AM FRUITFUL

The bible says:

"You did not choose me, but I chose you and appointed you so that you might go and bear fruit—fruit that will last—and so that whatever you ask in my name the Father will give you."

John 15:16 (NIV)

Sometimes I believe…

But this verse teaches me…

Prayer Points

God, thank you that...

God, please help me...

Doodle space

If you drew your thoughts, what would they look like?

YOU HAVE AN ETERNAL HOME

I HAVE AN ETERNAL HOME

The bible says:

"For we know that when this earthly tent we live in is taken down (that is, when we die and leave this earthly body), we will have a house in heaven, an eternal body made for us by God himself and not by human hands."

2 Corinthians 5:1 (NLT)

Sometimes I believe…

But this verse teaches me…

Prayer Points

God, thank you that…

God, please help me…

Doodle space

If you drew your thoughts, what would they look like?

About the author

I always had a faith in God. But who that God was – I wasn't sure?

I would pray as a child before going to bed, asking God to keep my friends and family, happy and healthy (amen!).

On two occasions, I remember outside speakers taking school assemblies to tell us something about Christian faith. One general; one specific to teenagers. The latter was particularly comical as I recall the presenter shouting "Nooooo!"" at the top of his lungs, as a suggested tactic to avoid sex before marriage.

As a teenager I had my act down. To the outside world I was confident, popular, and achieving. Internally I struggled with low-self-esteem, hidden unhealthy relationship with food, and feelings of being simultaneously too much for some people and not enough for others.

But on occasions like Easter and Christmas I would go to church with my cousins; Ruislip Baptist Church (RBC), a wonderfully warm church led by a charismatic and committed Geordie minister called Derek.

One Sunday evening, at RBC, Derek was baptising some adults from the church. As they shared their stories of knowing Jesus, God stirred my heart. He put a deep curiosity and hunger for whatever it was these people had and I wanted to know more.

At the end of the service Derek presented the gospel; he told me clearly and succinctly that I was made to be in relationship with Jesus, but my sin (bad choices, actions, and thoughts) had broken that relationship.

He told me that I needed to repent (say sorry) for my sin and give my life to Jesus, for Him to be Lord (like a Captain or Shepherd) and Saviour (my Rescuer from sin and a life without God). I secretly repeated his 'first steps' prayer in my head with an open heart to finding out more.

Not long after, I signed up for an Alpha course. My Mum was on a similar faith journey and had been on a course a few months before me and loved it, saying "you've got to come along".

Alpha, if you don't know already, is a course run by Christians worldwide, designed for people who want to explore the Christian faith. We'd eat together, watch a video, and then break into discussion groups which gave us the chance to ask anything(!).

I made a few arguments and asked all my questions. But ultimately that was the clarity I needed. God loved me – just as I was. So, several weeks later, I surrendered my life to Christ.

Since then, God has faithfully worked through the issues I held in my heart. He set me free by encountering His love and His Holy Spirit. He set me free from wrongful thinking and as a result I am passionate about sharing the truth of a Christian's identity in Christ with all believers.

So, I pray that you will encounter Jesus through this book. And will live in the freedom that Jesus won for you when he rose from the dead.

God bless, Kathryn x

.

Printed in Great Britain
by Amazon

75729368R00050